Sticky Faith Curriculum

FULLER YOUTH INSTITUTE
Can I Ask That?
8 Hard Questions about God and Faith
STUDENT GUIDE
A Sticky Faith Curriculum

Published in the United States of America by
Fuller Youth Institute, 135 N. Oakland Ave., Pasadena, CA, 91182
fulleryouthinstitute.org

ISBN 978-0-9914880-1-8

Cover and Interior Design: Matthew Schuler, Fuller Youth Institute
Cover Photo: Katie Swayze

Copy Editor: Joy Thompson
Printed in the United States of America

Student 6

CAN

HARD QUESTIONS ABOUT GOD & FAITH

I ASK

A STICKY FAITH CURRICULUM

THAT?

JIM CANDY, BRAD M. GRIFFIN, KARA POWELL

▽ Top tips for reading your Bible   ▽ Footnotes

Stephen was in his first week at college.

He was interested in a class he'd signed up for called "The Bible as Literature." The professor seemed really fun and obviously brilliant. Stephen figured she probably knew pretty much everything about the Bible.

"Welcome to class," Dr. Swanson smiled at the start of the opening session. "We're going to begin with Jonah."

The students stopped staring at their phones and looked up. It only took Stephen about ten seconds to notice the girl two chairs over from him. He *knew* there would be hot girls in college.

"Many of you have heard the Bible story of Jonah, a man who was swallowed by a big fish," Dr. Swanson continued. "But does anyone here actually *believe* that happened?"

Stephen looked around the class to see if anyone else would raise their hand. No one did and, most importantly, the hot girl kept her hand down ... so he didn't raise his hand either.

"Exactly," the professor continued. "There's no way Jonah could have been swallowed by a fish. It's just a literary device."

— — —

A literary device?

The professor explained how ancient writers used stories like this to illustrate a point. In fact, the prof continued, the story of Jonah was similar to *other stories* written by other ancient writers. Not only was it not a real story, but it was just a borrowed story from ancient fiction.

Inside, Stephen panicked.

Why didn't my youth leaders at church talk to me about this in high school? Were they hiding something? he wondered. *Is this professor telling the truth?*

As the prof continued, Stephen started wondering if the entire Bible fit the category she assigned to Jonah: *fiction*. He had always loved his church and Jesus as best he could, but his whole world was suddenly filled with doubt about his faith.

Surprised at himself, Stephen started to ask himself a deeper question.

Is faith in God something you do when you're a kid, just until you know better?

Yes you can ask $\boxed{1}$
that

The story above is an example of one of the many ways you might face new questions as you take your faith into the adult world.

It's probably not a surprise that many middle school and high school students deal with intense challenges to their faith. Some of those challenges come from outside, while others are doubts that sneak up from the inside. Maybe you've experienced some of both kinds of struggles yourself.

We've listened to the questions of teenagers like you, and we've written these sessions to explore openly the hot topics you take seriously or have questions about. These sessions will raise *tough questions* about your faith in God. The issues are challenging – so much so that some of the leading scholars in the world don't agree on their answers. The good news about that is you'll get to explore different viewpoints on some of Christianity's most avoided topics.

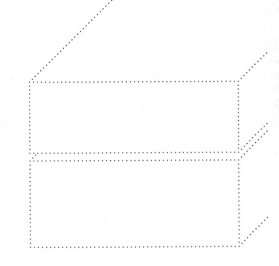

Most importantly, this study will help you think about what *you believe* in light of scripture and the insights of others. Belief is often something that changes and grows as you do. We hope you'll grow to trust Christ more as you wrestle with the hard questions we'll explore together:

The eight sessions tackle the following tough questions:

⊗ *Can I trust the Bible?*

⊗ *Does the Bible contradict itself?*

⊗ *Can I be a Christian and believe in evolution?*

⊗ *Does God discriminate against women?*

⊗ *Is Jesus really the only way to God?*

⊗ *What does the Bible say about being gay?*

⊗ *Does God endorse violence?*

⊗ *How can I follow a God who would let Christians do such bad things?*

2

What you should know
before you start

Here are a few important keys to help you along the way:

KEY #1:
This is about faith that sticks.

KEY #2: Don't hold back.

Sticky Faith is an initiative from the Fuller Youth Institute designed to understand and help faith "stick" in teenagers (see stickyfaith.org). In other words, we want to see young people grow in faith in Christ as they grow into adults. We have observed through research that wrestling with doubt—even doubt in God—can be a very healthy process. We hope this curriculum helps you have real conversations with God and each other about difficult topics.

ANY questions or doubts you have are welcome. In fact, they are required. Be honest. See what God might do with you—and in you—through this process. God is not biting fingernails, nervous about the tough questions you might ask. God is also not going to be angry or annoyed by doubt. Do not be afraid to use the words, "I don't know" in the face of tough questions. Those words acknowledge that we have a big God.

To understand what the Bible means, we need to understand *what it meant for the people who wrote and read it "way back then."* Studying the "context" means discovering who wrote the Bible, to whom they wrote, and why.

For example, imagine a friend of yours is in class and her phone buzzes. Someone texted your friend from a number she doesn't recognize:

I've been secretly wanting to ask you this for a while now ... Prom?

Because she doesn't recognize the number, she doesn't know whether to be excited or angry. The author and their intentions are unknown. Is it a friend playing a joke on her from someone else's phone? Is it the guy she dreams about? Was it sent to her accidentally?

Without the *context* of this mystery text message, she doesn't know what it means. The Bible is the same way. We need to know who wrote the passage (when possible), why they wrote it, and for what individual or community it was written. Context is crucial for understanding a passage. That's why most every session will have a section on "Context."

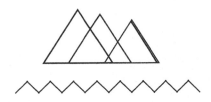

> **KEY #4: Don't study alone.**

These sessions should be studied with other people, not alone. One prayer for you is that you find adults who really care about you and about your faith journey. Some of you may not have someone older who invited you to study this together. If that's you, ask yourself, "Is there any adult I trust who loves Jesus?" Consider asking that person to help lead you in these sessions.

> **KEY #5: Ask God for help.**

These sessions will bring up challenging questions and potentially big breakthroughs for you. Jesus promises the Holy Spirit lives in us to help us make sense of the scriptures. Take God up on this promise, and ask the Holy Spirit to guide you as you begin this adventure!

Study *format*

- - -

△ *Sticky Story:* A relevant, realistic story designed to get teenagers talking, much like the one at the beginning of this introduction.

q *Sticky Questions:* Initial questions to unearth students' current opinions on the topic.

n *Sticky Notes:* A dialogue with background context and other factors that influence how people understand the issue. In this section we also share various and often opposing viewpoints within the Christian community or broader culture.

s *Sticking with the Scripture:* Relevant scripture and questions about each topic.

t *Sticky Talk:* Fictional conversations that capture the essence of the issue and opinions surrounding it.

Session

1

Can I trust the Bible?

Brett was the guy you never thought would walk away from God.

He was "Mr. Youth Group" – never missed a meeting, camp, or mission trip. EVERYTHING the church did, Brett was there. He even helped in the children's ministry and served as a camp leader.

He knew the Bible really well too. His parents had taught Brett a lot about the Bible, and he was one of those kids who seemed to get it. Most people thought Brett would become a pastor when he graduated from college.

But that all changed during Brett's senior year of high school.

Brett decided to write his final senior project on how the New Testament was written. He started searching the Internet for sources, and found a scholar who is well-known for his biblical knowledge. This scholar had written many books. Brett was thrilled to learn from someone this well respected on something he cared about so much.

As he read through the scholar's blog, he found a post that seemed like just what he was looking for. But as he read, Brett was surprised and somewhat concerned by the perspective shared by the author.

Has anyone played the game telephone? Telephone is the game when people pass a phrase around a circle by whispering into the next person's ear. Usually the message ends up very different by the time the phrase reaches the last person. Now, take a moment and imagine a giant game of telephone that lasts for centuries. That is the Bible.

Brett was intrigued. He had never thought about how the Bible was actually put together. He always just assumed the books of the Bible were all stored together in a museum somewhere.

"Now," the blog post continued, "I find it curious that some people actually bet their whole lives on a game of telephone." The next section was titled "The Truth about the New Testament" and listed all the reasons this writer believed the New Testament can't be trusted. [1]

Brett started wondering... *Am I betting my life on a telephone game?*

What he read on the blog ...

⊗   *We have no original copies of the New Testament books—only copies of copies.*

⊗   *The first copy we have of any part of the New Testament is from around the year 200 A.D.*

⊗   *People made mistakes when copying the Bible.*

⊗   *There are 300,000 changes in the Bible among all the different copies.*

q *(questions)*

What do you know already about how the New Testament was written? What have you heard?

By many people over a long period of time, books were chosen to be put in the bible.

Does it matter if the Bible has been significantly changed since its original letters and books were written? Why or why not?

If the same message as the original copy is still present, small changes wont really matter.

Read the blog notes again from the opening story. What if those notes were all true? What does this make you think? How does it make you feel?

1.
2. WB The old testament?
3. Human error is gonna happen.
4. Some things dont translate very well.

If you were in a conversation with this blogging professor, what would you say or ask? Why?

Can you show me proof of these "facts" and stats you've given as examples in your article.

What do you notice about what's written on the next page?

Paparus

Old
Hebrew/

New
Greek

Did Jesus know/learn how to
read & write

How would you guess something like this papyrus written 1,800 years ago became the Bible you have in your hand today?

By hard work & translation

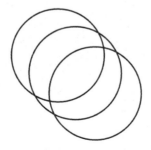

How do we know the version we use is the right one?

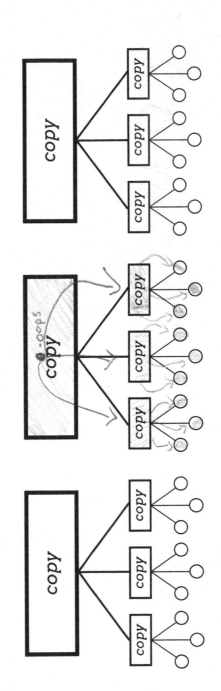

Original Greek Manuscript of each New Testament Book

 (notes)

Why does this matter?

Some people don't care if the Bible was changed through the years. They see it as a book with helpful thoughts from good teachers.

But the Bible is much more. The Bible contains the history of God and God's people over time, including the account of God actually coming to earth as a person: Jesus Christ.

 If the Bible has been *significantly* changed, it might be difficult to have confidence in the main messages of scripture about who God is and who we are.

How did we get the Bible we have today?

Although we believe the Bible is inspired by God, it didn't magically appear. God used normal people to write the Bible. Most scholars believe all the New Testament writings were completed within a handful of decades after Jesus' death and resurrection. The New Testament writers had access either to Jesus or to eyewitnesses of Jesus. People called "scribes" copied down the words of the Bible over many centuries.

> Did the scribes ever mess up? What goofs did they make?

CONTEXT!

Is it unusual that the Bible was copied by hand over the years? Answer: No.

Every ancient book was copied. Why? No photocopy machines or printing presses! The Bible has been copied by hand and eventually copied in print *more than any other book in history*.

Did every person who copied the Bible over the centuries do it with 100% accuracy? Few argue that every scribe did it perfectly and never made a mistake. The more important question is: What kind of changes (called *"variances"*) are there?

What Kinds of Changes Did Scribes Make?

There *are* examples of scribes making changes as they copied the texts.

Bart Ehrman, a widely recognized New Testament scholar (who does not claim to be a Christian), notes that the Bible has many "copy errors." However, Ehrman admits most differences don't significantly change the meaning of those texts:

"Most of these differences we have in our manuscripts are completely insignificant, unimportant and don't matter for a thing." [2] *- Bart Ehrman*

However, Ehrman believes some changes **do** affect how we read the Bible, like changes in the ways passages might be interpreted by shifting a word or two.

So are the scriptures we now have faithful to the "original" Bible texts or not?

It's a complicated question, but most Christian scholars agree the answer is YES. One problem with the "telephone" argument is that *we still have many of the early copies* that affirm later copies. Even if a scribe **did** make a mistake, we often have an earlier copy to compare. Another problem is that the biblical writings came out of primarily oral cultures, meaning people verbally shared stories in a whole different (and more consistent) way than we do today.

Why do we have so many translations now?

Different people have taken early manuscripts and attempted to translate the Greek words (or Hebrew in the Old Testament) into Latin, then later English and other languages. Also, over time the church came to agreement about which books were part of the authoritative Bible and which were not considered part of scripture. The Bible we have today is a product of those individuals, councils, Bible translators, and scholars through the years. But within the English language, for example, there are multiple translations of the Bible because different groups of scholars make different translation choices. That's because ancient languages often don't have exact English equivalents.

"The evidence for our New Testament writings is ever so much greater than the evidence of any writings of the classical authors, the authenticity of which no one dreams of questioning." [3]
— F.F. Bruce, New Testament Scholar (Bruce and other scholars are comparing the New Testament to classical works by authors such as Plato, Homer and Aristotle).

Father → Joseph

S  *(scripture)*

Most Christian traditions believe the Bible is God's inspired word to humanity. The Holy Spirit inspired human authors to capture God's Word and communicate it to God's people in specific places and times, as well as over time to us. Because we believe it's God's word, scripture has "authority" in our lives. The Holy Spirit uses scripture to shape us into people who live in relationship with—and try to live like—Jesus Christ.

The Bible is inspired by God for a *purpose*. Yes, it is designed to show us what happened and when. But it is also designed to *change us.* The apostle Paul wrote the following words prior to the creation of the entire New Testament we have today, but he still speaks to this reality when he writes:

Teaching & Training diff

There's nothing like the written Word of God for showing you the way to salvation through faith in Christ Jesus. Every part of Scripture is God-breathed and useful one way or another—(showing us truth, exposing our rebellion, correcting our mistakes, training us to live God's way.) Through the Word we are put together and shaped up for the tasks God has for us.

– 2 Timothy 3:15-17 (The Message)

Paraphrase

What do you think about the ways this passage claims the Bible is "useful"?

In what ways have specific Bible passages helped you to grow as a Christ-follower?

Job 11:18-19

How has the Bible been hard for you to understand?

Why do we need to know he liniage in the bible

(talk)

Pretend you are with some friends who start talking about God. Read their viewpoints and follow the instructions below.

WILL

I think Jesus is real and I don't understand why it matters if the Bible was changed or not. Almost everyone agrees that he was a real person and that he did amazing things. Why are we so worried over a few words in the Bible here and there? In fact, I'm not convinced that it really matters that Jesus was a real person. Can't we just live the way he taught us to live and not argue over a few changes in the Bible?

KIRSTEN

It's absolutely critical that the words in the Bible are the exact words of Jesus. If there is even one word that is not a direct quote, how can we trust that anything is accurate in the Bible? There are people out there who just don't like Christianity and are trying to make the Bible look bad.

MILES

All this study of the Bible is fine, but the big question is, "Would God allow us to have an unreliable record of his story?" God knew we would need a way to understand what it means to follow Jesus. I trust God enough to believe that we have the Bible we were supposed to get.

JESSICA

All these professors and scholars know way more than I do about the Bible. I have no idea how I'll ever tell what is right or wrong if the Bible was changed. So since I can't tell what is true or not, I am not sure if the Bible is true. How can anyone be totally sure? There are smart people who disagree on this stuff. Maybe they are all right and nobody is really wrong.

Instructions

- ⊗ Take a pencil or pen and *underline* any thoughts the characters shared that you agree with. Why do you agree?

- ⊗ Take a pencil or pen and *circle* the thoughts you disagree with. Why do you disagree?

- ⊗ Share with the group why you circled and underlined what you did. Be open to learning something here from your leaders and other group members!

Do you have any other questions right now about this topic? What are they?

My opinion on this topic (at least for now) is ...

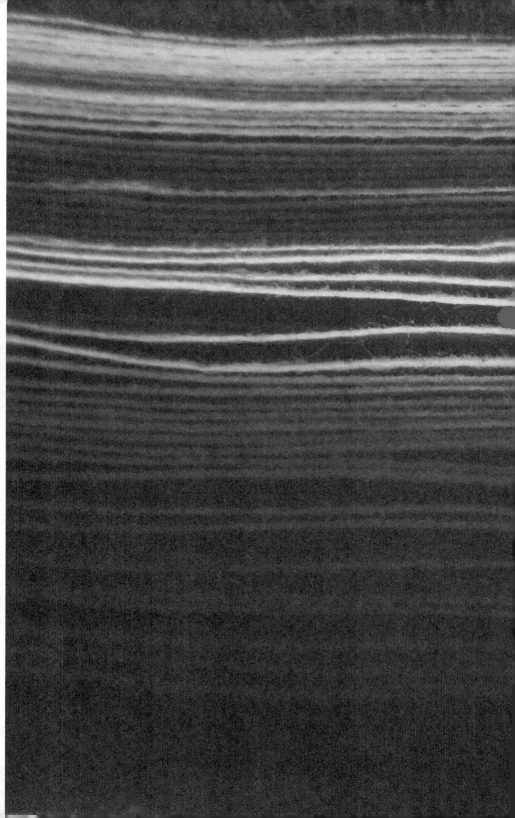

Session

2

Does the Bible contradict itself?

Ruth was friends with everyone.

People thought she was fun. Guys thought Ruth was cute. Her coaches thought she would get a scholarship in tennis. She was the "All American" kid. She was kind to other people too. Her teachers loved her. She got along with everyone.

Everyone but Annaliese.

Annaliese was quieter and not as well known at her high school, but she would ask Ruth questions that bugged her. Ruth didn't believe in God, and Annaliese was a Christian. Annaliese would often ask questions like, "If there is no God, what is life really about, Ruth?" Asking this once or twice was no big deal, but Annaliese would ask this question, or a version of it, often. Ruth thought it was annoying.

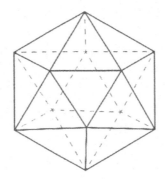

But sometimes it also made Ruth wonder. *Why don't I believe in God?*

Ruth's parents had always told her that the Bible was a book of nice stories, but once you studied it, you found out there were lots of contradictions. She decided to ask Annaliese about it.

"I have trouble believing God exists because I've heard the Bible gets its stories mixed up," Ruth said. "How can Christians say this book is from God when there are different accounts of the same story? I don't trust it."

"Where did you hear there are conflicting stories in the Bible?" Annaliese replied. "That's not true. Show me where."

So for a class project, Ruth decided to find contradicting passages in the Bible. She started with the resurrection of Jesus. *"If I can show Annaliese there are different accounts of the resurrection of Jesus, then I will finally win this ridiculous argument,"* she thought.

Ruth read Matthew, Mark, Luke and John's stories about Jesus' resurrection and found several discrepancies in the stories. She made the following chart for her class assignment to show the different ways each author wrote about the resurrection of Jesus.

Ruth shared her chart with Annaliese before she turned it in for her class. The chart surprised Annaliese. She went home and compared her Bible to Ruth's chart. It seemed to Annaliese there were differences after all.

Annaliese wondered, *Does this mean Ruth is right? Does the Bible have stories that don't agree with each other?*

What was Annaliese supposed to do with this new information?

	Matthew	Mark	Luke	John
Women who came to the tomb...	Mary Magdalene and the other Mary	Mary Magdalene and the other Mary	Mary Magdalene, the other Mary, & Joanna	Only Mary Magdalene
The tomb's entrance stone...	Angel appeared and rolled it away	Stone already had been moved	Stone already had been moved	Stone already had been moved
Angelic appearance...	Dressed in white – like lightning	Young man dressed in white	Two men like "lightning"	Two angels in white
The women felt...	Afraid but with great joy	Astonished and afraid; run away	Frightened	Mary doesn't seem afraid

(questions)

Why does this topic matter?

So that we can understand how people may use the bible against us

If you had a friend like Ruth who handed you this chart, what would you say or ask?

Do these differences change the story?

What did you learn from the stories?

How important is it to you that the Bible's authors agree 100 percent on every detail? Explain your answer.

Not very important for every little detail, because If they dont change The story If doesnt matter.

Who is a Christian you respect? What do they think about this topic? (Ask them this week before or after the group meets!)

My friend steff and my youth pastor.

n *(notes)*

Different perspectives

In court, witnesses give testimony. Often the accounts don't match. Does this mean nothing happened? Or could it mean they saw or heard the situation differently?

Jesus' resurrection story is an example of different writers giving their own views. Some people believe this actually *increases* the trustworthiness of the Bible because it shows the writers did not conspire to invent a perfect story. Further, the gospel writers were writing to different communities with different questions and concerns. They wanted to communicate not only *what* happened, but also *why* it was so important. Sort of like the way you tell a story differently when you're sharing it with your best friend or writing it for journalism class.

Inerrancy vs. Infallibility

Here are two fancy words describing how different people view the Bible's accuracy:

Inerrancy: This position holds that the Bible is without any factual error. The Bible is inspired by God and, therefore, all facts are completely accurate, even those that seem to contradict.

Infallibility: This position teaches that the Bible is inspired by God but may contain some factual or technical errors. However, those errors do not change the message of the Bible nor its purpose as God's authoritative Word to human beings.

Both perspectives believe in the authority of God's Word.

Luke was a doctor

These are not the only two ways to view the reliability of scripture, but two common ways that churches and individual Christians tend to interpret what they read.

> How else might someone explain differences between the stories of the Bible?

> What do you think is the main point of the resurrection story?

Do you think the different accounts shown in Ruth's chart weaken or strengthen that point, or make any difference given that main point?

Are there many other places where the writers' stories don't seem to fit together?

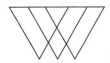

Here are a few other passages to check out:

* Read Matthew 27:3-8 and Acts 1:18-19 (two accounts of Judas' death)

* Read 1 Samuel 31:4-6 and 2 Samuel 1:6-10 (two accounts of Saul's death)

*A number of stories or parables of Jesus differ slightly or significantly among the four gospels. Try to find the same story in more than one of the gospels and look for any differences between them. For example, read the accounts of Jesus feeding 5,000 people in Matthew 14:13-21, Mark 6:30-44, Luke 9:10-17, and John 6:1-13.

CONTEXT!

When you read about a baseball game, the journalist often includes attendance figures. If it's the San Francisco Giants, the attendance is often around 42,031. These are *exact* numbers based on ticket sales.

Were Biblical writers as precise as modern writers? Or was the culture's take on recording numbers different? When the Bible says Jesus fed 5,000, did someone count? Or did they only count men, but not women and children? Or was the author just making the point that it was a *really big* crowd? The way you answer these questions is important; some believe the writers may not have been as concerned with exact detail as we are. Others disagree and believe God's inspiration means every detail is correct. Still others say the different writers were concerned about recording different things. (Ever read the book of Numbers? Open it now just for fun.)

As scribes were copying and recopying versions of the gospels, why wouldn't they have "cleaned up" the differences between the accounts of the gospel writers?

S   *(scripture)*

The beauty of the Bible is that God used ordinary people to write different parts of God's story—a story that would be shared for centuries. All of these writers were different, and had various reasons for writing down what they had seen or heard. Read Luke's take on why he wrote his version of the gospel to Theophilus and the community in which Theophilus lived:

> *Many have undertaken to draw up an account of the things that have been fulfilled among us, just as they were handed down to us by those who from the first were eyewitnesses and servants of the word. With this in mind, since I myself have carefully investigated everything from the beginning, I too decided to write an orderly account for you, most excellent Theophilus, so that you may know the certainty of the things you have been taught.*
>
> — Luke 1:1-4

Luke wrote this on papyrus paper. He didn't have a "cover page" or an editor, and there was no graphic designer to make it look cool. Often writers in ancient times would treat the opening sentence of a letter like we use the cover of a book today. They put really important information that they wanted to make sure people read and understood right at the front. So these first few sentences in Luke are important.

What is the main point of Luke's opening statement above?

What kind of confidence does that give you in the author's story?

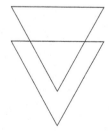

How to prove the bible is true without using the bible?

History Books yo!

What does it mean for *you* to be credible in how you share Jesus?

By the way you act. Do you live in Jesus?

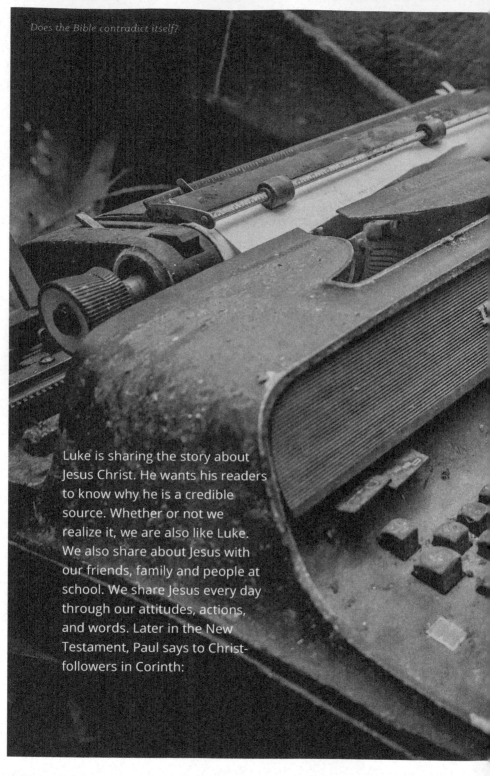

Luke is sharing the story about Jesus Christ. He wants his readers to know why he is a credible source. Whether or not we realize it, we are also like Luke. We also share about Jesus with our friends, family and people at school. We share Jesus every day through our attitudes, actions, and words. Later in the New Testament, Paul says to Christ-followers in Corinth:

You yourselves are our letter, written on our hearts, known and read by everyone. You show that you are a letter from Christ, the result of our ministry, written not with ink but with the Spirit of the living God, not on tablets of stone but on tablets of human hearts. — 2 Corinthians 3:2-3

(talk)

Pretend you are with some friends who start talking about God. Read their viewpoints and follow the instructions below.

TJ

I don't think the writers of the Bible were as concerned about every detail as we are today. Actually, I don't understand why some Christians think they have to prove the Bible has no contradicting stories. It actually makes people not want to be Christians. Smart people won't believe in God if they are forced to think some accounts don't actually contradict when they clearly do.

WRITE A QUESTION YOU'D LIKE TO ASK TJ:

_____

Nah

JESS

It's really important that every detail is correct in the Bible. God inspired it. Even if the authors of the Bible weren't worried about all the little details, God still helped them get it all right. The things that look like errors are not really errors at all. You can explain each of them pretty easily.

WRITE A QUESTION YOU'D LIKE TO ASK JESS:

_____

WILL

If the Bible has contradictions in it, how can you trust anything it says? If the writers have different stories about Jesus' resurrection, how do we know that it actually happened at all? It's popular right now to unfairly question the Bible. (If you don't accept every word of the Bible as directly perfect from God, how can you be a Christian?)

WRITE A QUESTION YOU'D LIKE TO ASK WILL:

_____

JULIE

Some Christians try to harmonize all the mistakes in the Bible. They take two different stories and they try to say they fit together somehow. Jesus' resurrection is an example. Don't try and make a story so that the different accounts all magically work together. Just admit they are different. It doesn't mean Jesus didn't rise from the dead.

WRITE A QUESTION YOU'D LIKE TO ASK JULIE:

_____

Talk with your group about why you asked the questions you wrote down above.

What other questions does this study raise for you about the Bible?

Session

3

Can I be a Christian and believe in evolution?

Tom couldn't sleep.

He kept replaying in his mind a conversation from his biology class earlier in the day. The topic was evolution, and he ended up becoming the center of attention.

"Evolution does not match up with the Bible." Mrs. Bronson had repeated that phrase at least five times during class that day. Tom liked Mrs. Bronson, but it was clear she didn't believe in God. "As a scientist and historian, I must inform you that that the Bible's version of how the world began is incompatible with science."

Mrs. Bronson split the class into groups to discuss Charles Darwin and evolutionary theories. Most people in Tom's high school knew he went to church. As soon as Tom got into his group with five other students, the questions began:

"You don't believe in evolution, do you Tom?"

"Sorry, but isn't it kind of ignorant to think the Bible is true when science so clearly contradicts the Bible?"

Tom didn't know what to say. He felt embarrassed and childish when the other students kept insisting science made faith in God irrelevant.

The irony is that Tom actually believed evolution *could* be true, but he believed God is real too. He was ashamed to admit his belief in evolution *and* God because his girlfriend, Jen, had a strong opinion about that.

"You can't believe in both evolution and God," Jen said. "The Bible says God created the world in six days and then rested."

"But couldn't it have been longer than six 24-hour periods?" Tom asked. He went back and read chapters one and two of Genesis. Tom wondered whether or not this was actually supposed to be a scientific account of creation.

"Why are you doubting God?" Jen replied. "You should have faith that what the Bible says is actually true. If you don't believe Genesis is true and that God did what it says in that book, how do you know that Jesus isn't just a fake story too?"

These conversations kept Tom awake at night. He started to wonder, *"If I believe in evolution and science, can I still be a Christian?"*

q *(questions)*

Have you ever experienced anything like the story above?

Always! Especially with My mother

In the beginning God created the heavens and the earth. Now the earth was formless and empty, darkness was over the surface of the deep, and the Spirit of God was hovering over the waters.

And God said, "Let there be light," and there was light. God saw that the light was good, and he separated the light from the darkness. God called the light "day," and the darkness he called "night." And there was evening, and there was morning—the first day.

— Genesis 1:1-5

Thus the heavens and the earth were completed in all their vast array.

By the seventh day God had finished the work he had been doing; so on the seventh day he rested from all his work. Then God blessed the seventh day and made it holy, because on it he rested from all the work of creating that he had done.

— Genesis 2:1-3

What do *you* think of the creation stories in Genesis 1 and 2? Are they written as precise historical accounts, poetic stories about how God created all things, or something else? Why do you think that?

Tom wondered, *can you be a Christian and believe in evolution?* What do you think of that question?

What does your church believe about this question? If you don't know ... take a guess.

 *(notes)*

Understanding "Biblical Interpretation"

Different people read or interpret the Bible in different ways. "Hermeneutics" (pronounced herm – uh – NOO – ticks ... say it a few times fast ... it's fun) is a fancy word for this. Interpretation is like the "lens" through which you read the Bible. We've already explored this process some in the last session.

Imagine taking a picture with a camera or your phone. The setting or filter you use can change how the picture looks—sometimes dramatically. Similarly, your experiences can affect your interpretation or "biblical hermeneutic." Everyone (even you!) has a hermeneutic. Your life has influenced you to read the Bible from a certain perspective. That's not a good or bad thing; it's just reality. And it's something to pay attention to as you read.

> Ok, that's nice... But what does hermeneutics have to do with evolution?

Literal and Figurative Interpretation of the Bible

Some people use a "literal interpretation" approach to scripture. A literal interpretation means Genesis 1 tells us the world was created in seven 24-hour periods.

"Figurative interpretation" takes the approach that some stories in the Bible may not be based on real historical events. They are stories that were created to make a point or tell a story, like Jesus' use of parables. A figurative interpretation of Genesis 1 might see it as a poetic story of God's creation of the world that was never intended to be scientifically accurate.

Christians Have Different Opinions on Biblical Interpretation

C.S. Lewis, who wrote the *Chronicles of Narnia* and some books on theology, believed not all biblical passages were meant to be literal. Some people in his day read the book of Revelation and were nervous that heaven would be boring. To that worry, Lewis wrote:

"... if they cannot understand books written for grown-ups, they should not talk about them. All the Scriptural imagery (harps, crowns, gold, etc.) is, of course, a merely symbolical attempt to express the inexpressible." [4]

Which approach do you tend to take – literal or figurative? Can you use both approaches to scripture? How?

Why do you think Lewis would make such a strong statement about interpreting the Bible?

John MacArthur, a well-known current-day pastor, believes in a more literal approach to reading scripture:

"Everything Scripture teaches about sin and redemption assumes the literal truth of the first three chapters of Genesis. If we wobble to any degree on the truth of this passage, we undermine the very foundations of our faith." [5]

Why does MacArthur say a literal approach to Genesis 1-3 is so important?

CONTEXT!

The ancient Biblical writers were a mix of poets, prophets, and historians. Therefore, some people believe their accounts of the beginning of the world—while inspired by God—were not meant to be taken *scientifically*.

Others disagree. They say God inspired the writers to know more than was humanly possible about what happened in the creation events. Their creation account is taken literally because it is directly from God. Even if they weren't trained scientists or even personally observed what they were writing about, God inspired them and all the details are scientifically accurate.

S   *(scripture)*

Even though there are differences between how people read the Bible, almost everyone agrees that not *every* word in the Bible is literal. For example, Jesus used many stories and examples to help make a point. The following passage is Jesus warning his followers about the danger of sin and how seriously we should treat things that pull us away from God:

> *If your hand or your foot gets in God's way, chop it off and throw it away. You're better off maimed or lame and alive than the proud owner of two hands and two feet, godless in a furnace of eternal fire. And if your eye distracts you from God, pull it out and throw it away. You're better off one-eyed and alive than exercising your twenty-twenty vision from inside the fire of hell.*
>
> —Mark 9:43-48, The Message

WARNING: PLEASE DO NOT TAKE THE SCRIPTURE
ABOVE 100% LITERALLY.

How many hands and eyes would you have if you took Jesus' command literally? I'm pretty sure you'd be left without hands, feet, or eyes. But don't worry—so would everyone else!

> What do you think is Jesus' main point in this passage?

> How does this relate to what we have been talking about?

Pretend you are with some friends who start talking about God.
Read their viewpoints and follow the instructions below.

ABBY

I think the Bible should be read literally. If you don't
read it for what it says, then how can someone determine
what is true and what is just story? It seems to me if
you don't think everything is literal, Jesus could just be
a made-up story too. I think you need to take the Bible
either "all or nothing." That's what faith is: trusting
God's word to be true, because God says it's true.

FERNANDO

I don't understand why the Bible has to be taken literally
at all. The writers of the Bible are writing fictional
stories with a point. Just because those stories didn't
happen doesn't mean the point isn't still the same. The
story of Jonah doesn't need to be true for me to believe
the point of the story: we need to love people who don't
love us.

BRETT

The Bible is something that takes effort and clear thinking
to really understand. Some passages should be taken
literally and others can be taken as more of a story. I
believe that Jesus was a real person, but I don't believe
that Genesis 1-3 is a literal story. Some stories in the
Bible sound like real stories to me, but others sound like
they were invented to make a good point. I'd rather focus
on what the point of the story is than argue over whether
it really happened or not.

JANELLE

I struggle to believe things that can't be verified by science. How can we know any of the stories and characters in the Bible to be true since we can't scientifically verify that they happened? I know a lot of Christians and think a lot of them are good people, but it doesn't make sense to me that they would base their lives on a book that is full of ancient stories with no science to back them up.

Which of these opinions is closest to yours?

Which of these opinions is furthest from yours? Why?

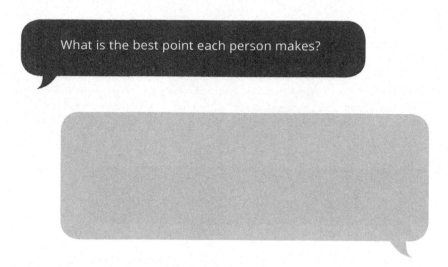

What is the best point each person makes?

Do you think the Bible should be read more literally or figuratively? Place an "X" on the line below to indicate where you stand right now. The left side is very literal. The right side is more figurative. Or you might feel like you're somewhere in the middle.

Literal   *Figurative*

Why did you put your X where you did?

Are there any other questions you have about this topic right now? Write them here, and if you're willing, share them with the group.

Session

4

Does God discriminate against women?

Dawn's friend Ty invited her to Sunday morning church.

Dawn decided to go, though she was way more interested in Ty than in the service itself.

But the morning surprised Dawn. Instead of a worship service with music and a talk, it was a meeting where the church was voting on the decision to hire a new pastor. Now that seemed like no big deal, but *everyone* was angry. People were yelling into a microphone about the new pastor and some were furious that the church was going to hire this person. Then Dawn found out why there was so much controversy.

The new pastor was a woman.

One person walked up to the microphone with a Bible in hand and said:

"How can we possibly be choosing a woman as our pastor? The Bible is clear that women should not be allowed to lead in that kind of role. 1 Timothy 2:11-14 says, 'A woman should learn in quietness and full submission. I do not permit a woman to teach or to assume authority over a man; she must be quiet. For Adam was formed first, then Eve. And Adam was not the one deceived; it was the woman who was deceived and became a sinner.'"

Dawn was shocked. Women can't teach? They're supposed to keep silent? She had no idea that passage was in the Bible. She wondered, *"Does being a Christian mean that I have to believe women are somehow inferior to men?"*

She decided to ask Ty about it.

"Women should let men lead," Ty replied. "I think that's not only true for church, but for families, too. The Bible says it clearly, and that's how our family works. My mom has never complained about it."

Dawn was confused. She didn't know she had to believe this in order to be a Christian.

q *(questions)*

Did you know the Bible has passages like the one quoted in our story? What do you know about those passages?

\- \- \-

What is your opinion NOW (before you go further in this study)? Do you think women should be allowed to serve in the church? What about in marriage and in the family? Why?

How much does this issue matter to you personally? Scale from 1-10?
1 = very little, 10 = LOTS! Why?

What does your church believe about women in leadership in the church or in marriage? If you don't know, take a guess!

n *(notes)*

CONTEXT!

It is important to know how women were treated during the time the New Testament was written, especially within Ancient Near Eastern culture. In general, women were not considered equal to men. For example, women were typically:

* Forbidden to talk to men (except their husbands)

* Not allowed to worship with men

* Forced to cover their heads, because hair was considered private

* Restricted to household work only

* Not considered reliable witnesses in a court of law

> Okay... How does all of this context affect how I read the Bible when it comes to women and men in leadership?

BONUS CONTEXT! (Lucky you...)

Some scholars believe Paul, who wrote the letter of 1 Timothy quoted in the opening story, intended this instruction specifically for Timothy and the people in Ephesus (the city where Timothy lived), but it is not necessarily meant for all places and all times. This position suggests that Paul was nervous that if women broke too many social norms (like teaching), people would reject Christianity—not because of Jesus, but because of the early church's countercultural view of women.

Other scholars and leaders believe Paul's words rise above a particular context and apply across cultures and centuries, much like the words of Jesus throughout the gospels. This is part of a bigger question about what in the Bible should be read as a "timeless truth" and what should be read as a teaching meant for a specific time, place, and people—or if there are such distinctions in scripture.

The Genesis Argument

The passage from 1 Timothy 2 in the opening story argues that Eve sinned first and therefore no woman should have authority over a man. This is sometimes called "The Genesis Argument." Here are two possible views Christians hold toward these verses:

1. Women should not lead men: Because 1 Timothy 2 refers to Genesis, many Christians believe this passage is not only relevant to Timothy and the Ephesians. The reference to Eve should be read as a general statement about all women. Therefore, it applies to our lives today.

2. Women should be able to lead men: Genesis shows that women carry out many of the same duties as men. For example, both women and men were asked to care for the garden, and both genders were created in the image of God with no apparent initial leadership differences. Therefore, women can be called by God to lead groups or churches that include men.

Church Leadership: Two BIG words

Complementarians generally believe men are the spiritual leaders of the church. Women can play important roles, but not lead men.

Egalitarians generally believe men and women are equal in the church, and members from either gender can lead.

It's important to note that many church traditions and individual believers fall somewhere between these big-worded positions. For example, a church or denomination might encourage women to lead certain ministries or even a church board, but not become ordained pastors. Or perhaps women can serve as associate pastors, but not as senior pastors.

If our society has changed a lot in the way we view women, should the church adapt too?

Examples of Women Leading in the Bible

Egalitarians might argue that, despite passages like 1 Timothy 2, there are also several examples in scripture of women showing leadership of various kinds. Here are some of those passages:

* *Miriam (Exodus 15)*
* *Deborah (Judges 4-5)*
* *Huldah* (2 Kings 22)
* *Anna (Luke 2)*
* *Priscilla* (Acts 18)
* *Phoebe, Junia, and others (Romans 16)*

> Now what about women and men in marriage and family relationships?

Home Leadership: Head and Helper or Equal Partners?

Some Christians believe God designed men and women with equal value but to play different roles, in particular in the husband-wife relationship and the leadership of the family overall.

This view holds that the husband's calling from God takes priority in life decisions and wives should support and help fulfill those decisions. For example, read Ephesians 5:22-23:

Wives, submit yourselves to your own husbands as you do to the Lord. For the husband is the head of the wife as Christ is the head of the church, his body, of which he is the Savior.

Other Christians think husbands and wives can have more egalitarian relationships in the home, dividing roles more according to gifts and skills, and making decisions together. Some of these folks might point to Ephesians 5 as well, but look more at verse 21 as the context for the rest: "Submit to one another out of reverence for Christ."

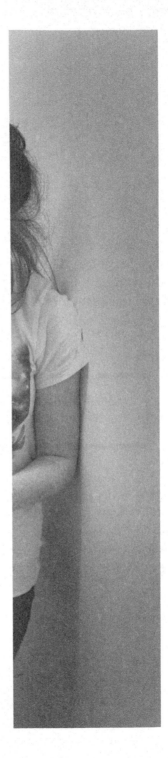

S (scripture)

It's important when you read a passage to get a sense of what the whole Bible says about that topic rather than make judgments based on only one verse or passage of scripture. The Bible may have things to say about that topic elsewhere too.

> **WARNING: DON'T LET ONE VERSE SPEAK FOR THE WHOLE BIBLE**

It's *always* a good idea to see what Jesus thought and did about something. Read the passage on the next page describing a woman who finds out Jesus is nearby and comes to see him. As you read it, think about parts of the story where you wonder if Jesus breaks a "cultural rule."

A woman in that town who lived a sinful life learned that Jesus was eating at the Pharisee's house, so she came there with an alabaster jar of perfume. As she stood behind him at his feet weeping, she began to wet his feet with her tears. Then she wiped them with her hair, kissed them and poured perfume on them.

When the Pharisee who had invited him saw this, he said to himself, "If this man were a prophet, he would know who is touching him and what kind of woman she is—that she is a sinner."

Jesus answered him, "Simon, I have something to tell you."

"Tell me, teacher," he said.

"Two people owed money to a certain moneylender. One owed him five hundred denarii, and the other fifty. Neither of them had the money to pay him back, so he forgave the debts of both. Now which of them will love him more?"

Simon replied, "I suppose the one who had the bigger debt forgiven."

"You have judged correctly," Jesus said.

Then he turned toward the woman and said to Simon, "Do you see this woman? I came into your house. You did not give me any water for my feet, but she wet my feet with her tears and wiped them with her hair. You did not give me a kiss, but this woman, from the time I entered, has not stopped kissing my feet. You did not put oil on my head, but she has poured perfume on my feet. Therefore, I tell you, her many sins have been forgiven—as her great love has shown. But whoever has been forgiven little loves little."

Then Jesus said to her, "Your sins are forgiven."

The other guests began to say among themselves, "Who is this who even forgives sins?"

Jesus said to the woman, "Your faith has saved you; go in peace."

— Luke 7:37-50

These quick notes of context may help:

* A woman labeled "sinner" was likely a prostitute or adulterer.

* If someone talked to a "sinner," that person was considered "unclean," meaning they couldn't participate in religious gatherings or rituals.

* The Pharisees were the ultra-religious types who wanted to make sure religious laws were never broken.

* Women often did not even speak in the presence of men in any public place.

* Feet were considered one of the dirtiest parts of a person. It was unusual to touch another's feet.

* Women's hair was considered private, even sexual.

How does Jesus surprise you in this passage?

How does this passage speak to Jesus' view of the value of this woman?

What other biblical passages affect our understanding of women's value in God's eyes?

What about passages that say something about women in leadership or in family relationships?

(*talk*)

Take a moment to pretend you are at college, or in the military, or at your job and are with some of your new friends who start talking about God. Read the viewpoints below and follow the instructions.

Mark ⊕ if you agree, ⊖ if you do not agree, and ⊙ for neutral.

SAM

I don't think women should be angry about not being allowed to lead in the church. They have a different role to play that is just as important. It's just not leadership. If both women and men could accept the roles that God has created for them, the church would be better off.

JILL

I hate that the Bible says women shouldn't lead in the church, but the Bible is what I follow, even if I don't like it. Even though I'm gifted in leading, I won't do it because I trust the Bible. Sometimes there are things in the Bible that we don't understand, but we have to trust God because God has a better perspective than we do.

MIGUEL

The Bible actually is one of the most liberating books ever for women. The way Jesus treated women totally gave them more freedom. There are many passages where women are given positions of leadership and the Bible makes it clear they are equal to men. The passages that seem not to allow women in leadership were actually just written for the first century context. They don't apply to us today.

KARIN

I think the Bible is wrong in its stance on women. There are some things written in the Bible that I can't accept. I know some people say that we should accept everything the Bible says, but in this case, I don't think it's right to agree with the Bible. Passages like the one in 1 Timothy have been used to harm women for years. No matter what the Bible says, I refuse to agree with it if it hurts someone.

You should have circled one of the three buttons after each person above. Why did you choose the button you chose?

One more thing I'd like to say about this topic is ...

Is Jesus really the only way to God?

Session

5

Jamal and Chris had always been friends, but their arguments were getting personal.

"I feel like you're saying that I am going to hell," Chris said with anger. His conversations with Jamal about God had been light-hearted up until now, but Chris was tired of Jamal making him feel like his Mormon faith was inadequate.

"I'm sorry, but I think Mormonism is wrong, Chris," Jamal answered. "And it's not for me to decide who is going to heaven and who is going to hell—only God does that. But I believe that the only people who will be with God forever are those who believe Jesus is Lord."

"But I do believe in Jesus," Chris responded.

"Not the same way that I do," Jamal replied.

Chris and Jamal decided not to talk to each other for a couple of days. When they saw each other again, it was over lunch with some other friends. Susannah, who claimed to be "kinda Jewish," joined in the conversation.

"I don't understand why you're arguing about which religion is better," Susannah said. "The only thing that matters is that you believe in some version of God and be a loving person. All religions are basically the same idea but with different names."

"I agree with Susannah," Martin added as he plopped down beside them with his lunch. "This is exactly why the world will never have peace. Religious fights will never help us get along with each other."

Jamal had heard at his church that he needed to be committed to Jesus and Jesus alone. But he didn't know how to respond to Chris, Susannah or Martin.

How should I think about my friends' faith? he wondered to himself. *Am I being too closed-minded about religion?*

q   (questions)

Have you ever been part of a story like this?
What happened?

> What do you think of Susannah's and Martin's comments in this story? Who do you agree or disagree with more? What would you say?

Susannah - Agree
If Its only based on being good, most of the world to fail.

What do you think of the way Jamal handled himself in this story?

I think he handled himself wrong because he wasful scaring his forend into his religion.

How do you think Jamal is doing when it comes to sharing his faith with "gentleness and respect" (1 Peter 3:15-16)? How important do you think that is?

How were you raised in your family to think about salvation and the difference among religious faiths?

"only one one way to God and thats through Jesus"
"you must respect others religions"

What does your church believe about salvation and the difference among religious faiths?

 (notes)

Do all religions see Jesus the same? Here is a table showing different viewpoints about Jesus' identity, purpose, and resurrection from the dead. These are only a few of the world's religious traditions, but ones you might have come across in the U.S. or your own community.

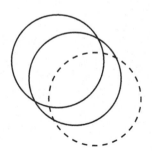

Who?
Muhammed.

Religious Tradition	Christianity	Islam	Judaism	Buddhism	Mormonism
Who was Jesus?	Both God and human. As part of the Trinity, he is the savior of human beings.	A human being who was a prophet of God, but not as great as the prophet Muhammad.	A human being, but not the Messiah (King, or Savior) Jews are waiting for.	A good person, but not God. There is no "God."	He was a human being at first, but later he became a god.
Why did he come?	To rescue human beings from sin by the gift of grace, to show us how to live in right relationship with God & the world.	He came to show God's (Allah's) will for people.	A rabbi who falsely claimed to be the Messiah & fulfill scripture. Jesus not mentioned in any sacred texts.	Jesus came to help people who need enlightenment.	A god & example for us. Human beings may also attain the status of being a god by following Jesus' example of love & sacrifice.
Was Jesus resurrected from the dead?	Yes.	No.	No.	No. Buddhists believe in reincarnation, or coming to life as another being after death.	Yes.

Core value

105

Which differences in the religions listed in the diagram do you think are most important?

Word to know: *Religious Pluralism* is the belief that all religions are equally valid. Religious pluralists believe that even though some religions might contradict each other, each holds a part of the eternal truth of the Divine.

John Hick, a well-known proponent of religious pluralism, teaches, "Applying a kind of philosophical Golden Rule, it would be unreasonable not to grant to religious experience within other traditions what I affirm of it within my own tradition."

most open minded
↓ cuz anyone can be one

Are Christians "Narrow Minded"?

Tim Keller, pastor of Redeemer Presbyterian Church in New York City, writes, "It is no more narrow to claim that one religion is right than to claim that one way to think about all religions (namely that all are equal) is right." Keller is saying that any stance we take—whether it's Christianity or religious pluralism—inherently prefers one perspective over others. In other words, there's nothing essentially "narrow minded" about believing that Jesus is the only way to God.

Do we have a "jealous" God?

Read Exodus 20:4-6 and the story in Exodus 32:1-14.

> Why would God ever be "jealous"?

"God's Jealousy is positive?"
"Worship of any thing is harmful"
"Holy Jealousy" ex)protecting marriage.

■ ▬ ■

(*scripture*)

One of the most radical claims Jesus made comes from John 14. As Jesus is talking to his disciples and is preparing to be killed and then rise again from the dead, he says:

make or break our faith

"Do not let your hearts be troubled. You believe in God; believe also in me. My Father's house has many rooms; if that were not so, would I have told you that I am going there to prepare a place for you? And if I go and prepare a place for you, I will come back and take you to be with me that you also may be where I am. You know the way to the place where I am going."

Thomas said to him, "Lord, we don't know where you are going, so how can we know the way?"

Jesus answered, "I am the way and the truth and the life. No one comes to the Father except through me. If you really know me, you will know my Father as well. From now on, you do know him and have seen him."

— John 14:1-7

one way.

> What does Jesus mean when he says he is the "Way"? the "Truth"? the "Life"?

Jesus is the true way to g[o] [t]o eternal life.

—

Thor
analogy

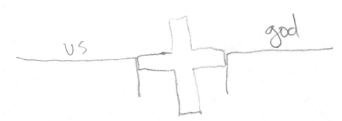

US   god

Underline what is said in the previous passage that might impact how we view religious pluralism.

If there were other ways for human beings to be in a right relationship with God, why did Jesus die on a cross?

Galatians 2

Look up : Personality

Respond to this statement: "Religious pluralism destroys the personality of God."

Personality of God Important!

What do you think Jesus means in Revelation 21:5 when he says, "I am making everything new"? If Jesus' mission is to restore all things, how do we live in a way that points to that kind of hope?

Clensing sin.

Be that example. Give them a reason to question and learn more about God

 *(talk)*

Pretend you are with some friends who start talking about God. Read their viewpoints and follow the instructions below.

ELI

Faith is a personal thing. I will always respect what you believe. All I'm asking for in return is that you respect what I believe. To say that my religious beliefs are false is intolerant. I think Jesus is a wonderful example, but there are other ways to find great truth too. We should affirm each other's belief in God and stick together so we can bring good to the world.

CARLA

Jesus is the center of my life and faith. I'm not concerned about getting into arguments with people, but I do believe Jesus is the true way to know God. Jesus told us to make disciples, so I will spend my life trying to help other people know him. People will know Jesus by the way I love others and it's important to share Jesus whenever I can so that everyone can know the truth.

SCOTT

We need to fight for Jesus in today's world. Everyone is so afraid of offending other people that we lose a sense of what makes us different and unique. Christianity *is* different than other faiths, and I believe we need to make sure people know what those differences are. People might call me intolerant, but aren't they just being intolerant of me too?

SARAH

4 Christians I know who claim to know all the truth make me so mad. How can they be so arrogant? What about people who were born in cultures where they grew up learning a different faith? How can we be so convinced that they aren't right too? I believe in Jesus, but I respect the rights of anyone to believe what they think is correct about God.

Rank these views from 1-4 (#1 is the view you most agree with). Why did you rank them in that order?

Placing yourself in this conversation, how can you talk respectfully with these friends about their beliefs while also expressing your own?

What are you still wondering about when it comes to this topic?

Session

6

What does the Bible say about being gay?

Christina and Johanna grew up going to church together.

They went to camp in the summer, sat together at church on Sunday mornings, and memorized the same verses in the Bible Memory Contest in 3rd grade.

Christina and Johanna remained friends through middle school and into high school. Christina's first boyfriend was in 7th grade. She would meet him after school and they would walk downtown together. He was the first of many boyfriends for Christina.

Johanna, on the other hand, never had a boyfriend. Because they were pretty close friends, Christina would joke with her about it sometimes.

"Why don't you go for Nolan?" Christina would tease. "You'd be perfect together."

Johanna would usually change the subject.

Partway through their junior year, Christina noticed that Johanna stopped coming to church.

"Why haven't you been at church lately?" Christina asked one day.

"I just have too much to do," Johanna responded. "I'm buried in homework all the time."

Christina understood what it was like to be busy, so she didn't think much of it. But there was something else going on with Johanna that Christina didn't realize. Finally, toward the end of their junior year, Johanna decided to tell Christina her biggest secret.

One night while they were out grabbing some dinner together, Johanna told Christina that she had something important to share.

"Christina, I think I'm gay."

At first, Christina didn't know what to say. She was confused because she'd known Johanna so long and never would have guessed she was gay.

Johanna also explained that this was why she had stopped coming to church. "I know God doesn't approve of me anymore," Johanna said. "There is no way I can ever go back now."

Christina wondered, *Is it wrong to be gay and Christian? What does the Bible say about that?*

(questions)

Why do you think Johanna is afraid to come back to church? Should she be afraid? Why or why not?

What would you say to Johanna? From your perspective, how has the LGBT (Lesbian, Gay, Bisexual, Transgender) community been treated by Christians?

How does your church talk about sexual identity and faith?

- Scriptural teaching of sexuality
- Live in purity in sexuality
- Sexual relation between man & women
- Sin has effected sexuality
= God is priority!

- Like other sins, sexual sins are forgiven

find throughout bible.

n (*notes*)

THE BIBLE ON HOMOSEXUALITY

Some of the passages that address homosexuality in the Bible are Leviticus 18:22, Leviticus 20:13, 1 Corinthians 6:9-11, and 1 Timothy 1:8-10. Take a few minutes to read each passage. We'll discuss another passage in Romans 1 later.

CONTEXT!

Some scholars claim that one or more of these passages may not directly constitute a condemnation of LGBT practices, but instead are contextual to what was happening in those specific places and cultures when these parts of the Bible were written. For example, same-sex prostitution was practiced in some ancient religions. People who argue that the Bible does not prohibit homosexuality say these passages are actually addressing prohibitions against same-sex prostitution common to those religions.

Others believe the passages teach that God designed people only for relationships with the opposite sex. They also note that Jesus always taught about marriage in the context of male and female relationships, never in the context of same-sex relationships.

Leviticus 18:22 - NO gay sex, Its a sin

Leviticus 20:13 - Death from sa gay sex.

Corinthians 6:9-11 -

Those who do gay sex will not inherit kingdom of heaven but! youre forgiven -

SLAVES, WOMEN, AND HOMOSEXUALS

A book by former pastor and professor <u>Dr. William Webb</u>
notes that the Bible tends to go against the cultures of its
time in these three areas in particular. Here is his argument
in a nutshell: [12]

	Slavery	*Women*	*Homosexuality*
The Culture During the Time of the Bible	The culture accepted slavery. Slaves had no rights.	Women had no rights and had many restrictions placed on them.	Homosexuality was widely accepted during this time period.
The Bible's Response	The Bible goes against culture by advocating rights for slaves.	Subverts culture by granting new freedoms. Jesus radically treated them as equals.	The Bible goes against culture – homosexuality is not mentioned positively. Jesus is silent on the issue.
What It Might Mean for Today	The Bible's teaching is used as a rationale to abolish slavery.	Many use the Bible's teaching as reasoning for full equality of women.	The Bible moves toward freedom for slavery & women's issues, but does not move toward an embrace of homosexuality.

1 Timothy 1: 8-10
Law is for those who sin.

- - -

Do you understand Webb's argument? With what do you agree? With what do you disagree?

Why is homosexuality emphasized so much? Some Christians are asking the question, "If Jesus never addressed homosexuality, why has this become such a big issue to some churches?" How would you respond to that question?

Some Christian groups like to argue
So they use Homosexualities
against others. Christians are
called to Love. God hates sin
not the sinne
Be like Jesus,
Gay is Sin But
you're forgiven

VIOLATING THE ORIGINAL
COMMANDMENT TO HUMAN BEINGS?

Many who say the Bible is clear in its affirmation of male and female relationships alone point to the original command given to human beings to "be fruitful and multiply" (Genesis 1:28). This multiplication is not biologically possible in same-sex relationships. Others note that leaning on this passage alone also implies that single people or married people without children are sinning because they are not "multiplying."

Can someone have feelings of same-sex attraction without being gay?

Yes!
Attraction, Lust, Sexual activity.
Taking it further than thought
is the sin.

What points on this Sticky Notes page do you find most important? Why?

What should someone do if the Bible teaches something they disagree with?

Trans?/Pan?

S (*scripture*)

Romans 1:18-32 is the New Testament passage frequently cited in arguments that the Bible places homosexuality outside of God's best plan for human beings.

> *The wrath of God is being revealed from heaven against all the godlessness and wickedness of people, who suppress the truth by their wickedness, since what may be known about God is plain to them, because God has made it plain to them. For since the creation of the world God's invisible qualities—his eternal power and divine nature—have been clearly seen, being understood from what has been made, so that people are without excuse.*
>
> *For although they knew God, they neither glorified him as God nor gave thanks to him, but their thinking became futile and their foolish hearts were darkened. Although they claimed to be wise, they became fools and exchanged the glory of the immortal God for images made to look like a mortal human being and birds and animals and reptiles.*

Therefore God gave them over in the sinful desires of their hearts to sexual impurity for the degrading of their bodies with one another. They exchanged the truth about God for a lie, and worshiped and served created things rather than the Creator—who is forever praised. Amen.

Because of this, God gave them over to shameful lusts. Even their women exchanged natural sexual relations for unnatural ones. In the same way the men also abandoned natural relations with women and were inflamed with lust for one another. Men committed shameful acts with other men, and received in themselves the due penalty for their error.

Furthermore, just as they did not think it worthwhile to retain the knowledge of God, so God gave them over to a depraved mind, so that they do what ought not to be done. They have become filled with every kind of wickedness, evil, greed and depravity. They are full of envy, murder, strife, deceit and malice. They are gossips, slanderers, God-haters, insolent, arrogant and boastful; they invent ways of doing evil; they disobey their parents; they have no understanding, no fidelity, no love, no mercy. Although they know God's righteous decree that those who do such things deserve death, they not only continue to do these very things but also approve of those who practice them.

Here are two viewpoints (among many) on this passage:

Viewpoint #1: This passage makes it clear that God designed males and females for relationships with each other. Anything outside of that is unnatural according to how God created human beings. God brings judgment against people who commit sexual sin.

Greek Influence

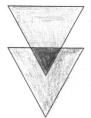

Viewpoint #2: This passage is addressing the Hellenistic culture as practiced by Romans of Paul's time that promoted worship of many gods. As part of their worship, first-century Romans practiced homosexual rituals. This passage is not speaking against LGBT people in general; it is speaking against the worship practices of that pagan culture.

What do you think is the point of this passage? If you were going to write your viewpoint (which could be #1 or #2, or something different), what would you say?

#2 but also #1

This passage talks about "natural" relations. Do you believe sexual orientation is something people are born with? Why or why not? How does that factor affect this conversation?

We are born sinfull
We gravitate.
We go toward a sin

Pretend you agree with the first viewpoint above. Why do you think people with the second viewpoint believe what they do?

Now swap your views and pretend you agree with the second viewpoint. Why do you think people who hold the first viewpoint believe what they do?

t *(talk)*

Pretend you are with some friends who start talking about God and sexuality. Read their viewpoints and follow the instructions below.

MONIQUE

I believe in the Bible but don't think the passages really prohibit being gay as we know it today. But there are other Christians I respect who disagree with me. I think being gay is okay because it is not hurting anyone else. Jesus never really talks about it. Don't you think that if it were really wrong, Jesus would have said something about it? *Good point*

CARLOS

The culture is sliding more and more away from God, and its view on LGBT issues is just one more example. The Bible is clear in lots of places that being gay is wrong. It scares me that people are choosing to say they are Christians and yet they will not take the Bible seriously on this issue. I do not believe practicing gays can be in a right relationship with God. *Wow Carlos...*

TANYA

The scripture seems clear to me that God's best plan is that only men and women should be together in sexual relationships. I'm always learning about this and I'm willing to talk to people who believe differently than me. But Jesus' teaching on marriage and the first marriage in creation seem clear that this was God's intent. It breaks my heart, though, that anyone who is gay would ever feel like they are rejected.

ALAN

Jesus would never be against gay people if he were alive today. He was the most loving person ever to live. Any church that discriminates against gays and lesbians is living in ancient history. This is exactly why people don't believe in God anymore. It's because the church has become so narrow-minded and judgmental. I want to make sure the church becomes open and affirming to all people, LGBT or otherwise.

Who do you most want to have a conversation with about this topic? What would you say or ask next?

Who do you most agree with above?
Write a few sentences explaining why.

What other questions are still bugging you about this topic?

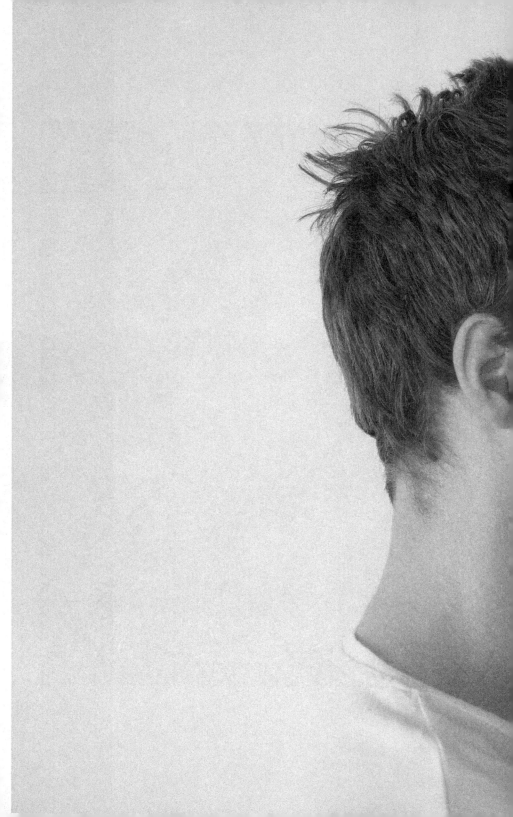

Session

7   Does God endorse violence?

Lilly grew up in her church's children's ministry.

By the time she was in 4th grade, she had heard every children's version of a handful of Bible stories, but she didn't really start reading the Bible for herself until she was a senior in high school. Having only read the Gospels and Psalms all the way through before, she decided to start at the beginning in Genesis.

When Lilly was a kid, she had loved the Noah's Ark story. It gave her something to do with her stuffed animal collection. But now that she was reading it for herself from the "real" Bible, she realized her Sunday School teachers left out a few parts of the story that are a little less warm and fuzzy. Parts like this:

"The LORD saw that the wickedness of humankind was great in the earth, and that every inclination of the thoughts of their hearts was only evil continually. And the LORD was sorry that he had made humankind on the earth, and it grieved him to his heart. So the LORD said, "I will blot out from the earth the human beings I have created – people together with animals and creeping things and birds of the air, for I am sorry that I have made them. But Noah found favor in the sight of the LORD."
- Genesis 6:5-8 (NRSV)

A bit later, all the animals piled onto the massive boat two-by-two and sailed away into the most fun floating petting zoo the world has ever seen. But the story was different for those who weren't on the boat:

"All flesh died that moved on the earth, birds, domestic animals, wild animals, all swarming creatures that swarm on the earth, and all human beings; everything on dry land in whose nostrils was the breath of life died."
- Genesis 7:21-22 (NRSV)

▬   ▬   ▬   ▬   ▬

So while the giraffes snuggled together on the Ark, thousands of human beings (it's actually hard to say exactly how many) were being swept away in a devastating storm.

Lilly thought about that. *"All flesh died."* Dads, moms, children ... all gone.

She noticed the Bible makes it clear that this was *not* a random natural disaster like an unforeseen tsunami or a nasty tornado. This was a storm *brought on by God.*

She kept reading and noticed that the Old Testament tells more stories of God's destruction.

God destroyed the cities of Sodom and Gomorrah with "sulfur and fire" from heaven (Genesis 19), and later swallowed the entire Egyptian army in the Red Sea so that "not one of them remained" (Exodus 14), after having just killed every firstborn son in every family in Egypt. In 1 Samuel 15, the prophet Samuel commands Saul on behalf of God saying, "Go, attack the Amalekites and totally destroy all that belongs to them. Do not spare them; put to death men and women, children and infants, cattle and sheep, camels and donkeys.'" Kill them all and don't spare

anyone – *even their babies*? The Amalekites were a neighboring country; what happened to that whole "love your neighbor" thing?

Lilly began to wonder, *"What kind of violent and bloodthirsty God is this?"*

q (*questions*)

Have you ever heard anyone say they can't believe in a God who is violent? What was that conversation like for you?

If we *only* had the story of Noah for context, what would you say about the character of God?

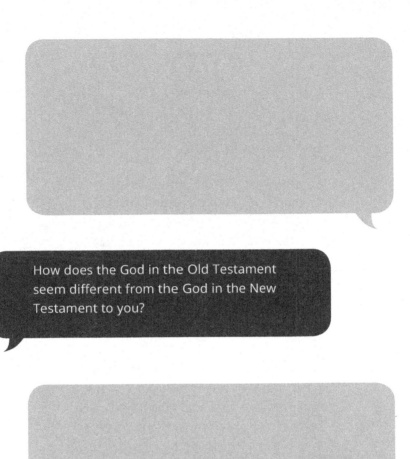

How does the God in the Old Testament seem different from the God in the New Testament to you?

 *(notes)*

Other Viewpoints

Some have pondered stories like Noah's Ark and concluded that God is not good. Here are a couple of famous people who decided against following God, in part based on stories like Noah's.

Thomas Paine, an American revolutionary and author of *Common Sense* and *The Age of Reason*:

"Whenever we read... the cruel and tortuous executions, the unrelenting vindictiveness with which more than half the Bible is filled, it would be more consistent that we call it the word of a demon than the word of God. It is a history of wickedness that has served to corrupt and brutalize mankind; and, for my part, I sincerely detest it, as I detest everything that is cruel." [6]

Richard Dawkins, a renowned atheist:

"The God of the Old Testament is arguably the most unpleasant character in all fiction: jealous and proud of it; a petty, unjust, unforgiving control-freak; a vindictive, bloodthirsty ethnic cleanser..." [7]

How would you respond to Thomas Paine's and Richard Dawkins' opinions?

The Bible is Usually Raw

The Bible doesn't always soften things to make God or people who follow God look good. In many cases, the Bible simply tells the story and leaves us wondering. We witness the incredible love, grace, pain, mistakes, and yes, even blood, of real life. The Bible sometimes gives us all the gory details while leaving out answers to questions that we wish could be neatly resolved.

CONTEXT!

Many of the stories of the Old Testament take place in very brutal cultures. Few tribes and people groups had real laws. For the most part, people did whatever they wanted (or whatever their gods wanted), which included all kinds of ruthless violence. Over time, God led the Israelites to be *far more civilized* (in the ways people were treated) than surrounding nations.

For example, remember the Amalekites mentioned in the opening story (1 Samuel 15)? God didn't want the people of Israel to marry into their people and have children. Why? Like many other cultures around Israel, they had some nasty practices like sacrificing their own infants to their gods (you read that right) and killing women who were pregnant. These were not practices that aligned with the way God wanted his people to live.

God Responds to Sin

One thing is consistent about all the hard stories of the Old Testament: God never acts randomly. God acts against people doing wrong. As hard as it is to read some of the Old Testament stories, imagine a world where God never took action. What if God didn't care that the Amalekites were sacrificing their children? Is that the kind of God you'd want to follow?

God's Unlikely Love and Patience Seem to be EVERYWHERE in the Old and New Testaments

The Bible is filled with stories of God's patience and love. Over and over again, God loves people who don't deserve it. Jonah is a great example. It's tempting to focus on the sleepover in the fish belly, but don't miss the rest of the narrative. God asked Jonah to go to Nineveh (a city considered very anti-God at the time) and invite them to follow God. Jonah didn't like that idea and tried to go as far away as possible – to a place called Tarshish. When God finally led him to Nineveh, Jonah was still upset. He *hated* the people there. Even after they responded to the message and turned away from evil, Jonah was ticked. Don't believe us? Check this out:

> *Jonah was furious. He lost his temper. He yelled at GOD, "GOD! I knew it—when I was back home, I knew this was going to happen! That's why I ran off to Tarshish! I knew you were sheer grace and mercy, not easily angered, rich in love, and ready at the drop of a hat to turn your plans of punishment into a program of forgiveness!* — Jonah 4:1-2 (The Message)

Read those two verses again carefully. The words *"I knew it..."* are really important. Despite the fact some want to portray God as cruel, comments like Jonah's make it clear God had a reputation for loving people who didn't deserve it. This becomes even more evident when Jesus comes on the scene.

Which of these points do you think is most important on this topic? Why?

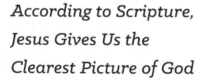

According to Scripture, Jesus Gives Us the Clearest Picture of God

In Colossians 1, Jesus is described as the "visible image of the invisible God." Jesus was God himself, who came to earth as a human being or, as some like to say, he was "God in the bod." That means whenever he opens his mouth or reacts to a situation, *you get to see God in action.* If you want to know God, know Jesus. So the question then becomes, "Is Jesus violent?"

Which of these points do you think is most important? Why?

S   *(scripture)*

Many people in the first century expected, based in part on the stories from the Old Testament, that Jesus would lead a military campaign to defeat the Romans (who had taken over Israel). They expected a rebellion headed by an amazing fighter. What they got instead was a God who chose to be born in humble circumstances in the middle of nowhere. Jesus grew up in a common family of his time, helping to build furniture to survive. While many religious people of the day expected a great warrior, God came to earth in a way that no one expected – as a poor, compassionate carpenter-turned-teacher named Jesus. He lived and loved people in a way that, according to the gospel of Mark, announced the Kingdom of God (Mark 1:15). This kingdom would be different than the kingdoms of earth. When the time came that some people in power wanted Jesus dead, the creator of the universe had a choice: would he use his unlimited power to destroy his enemies? Or would he lay his power aside and allow himself to be sacrificed?

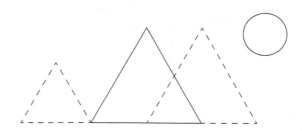

While he was still speaking, Judas, one of the Twelve, arrived. With him was a large crowd armed with swords and clubs, sent from the chief priests and the elders of the people. Now the betrayer had arranged a signal with them: "The one I kiss is the man; arrest him." Going at once to Jesus, Judas said, "Greetings, Rabbi!" and kissed him.

Jesus replied, "Do what you came for, friend."

Then the men stepped forward, seized Jesus and arrested him. With that, one of Jesus' companions reached for his sword, drew it out and struck the servant of the high priest, cutting off his ear.

"Put your sword back in its place," Jesus said to him, "for all who draw the sword will die by the sword. Do you think I cannot call on my Father, and he will at once put at my disposal more than twelve legions of angels? But how then would the Scriptures be fulfilled that say it must happen in this way?"

In that hour Jesus said to the crowd, "Am I leading a rebellion, that you have come out with swords and clubs to capture me? Every day I sat in the temple courts teaching, and you did not arrest me. But this has all taken place that the writings of the prophets might be fulfilled." Then all the disciples deserted him and fled.

— Matthew 26:47-56

What is Jesus' reaction toward violence in this passage?

Assume for a moment that Jesus was all-powerful and could have wiped out the Romans with his angel army (by the way – a legion is 6,000 soldiers. Do the math: that's a lot of angels). Why didn't he do it?

What does this passage tell you about God's character?

What other stories from the New Testament give us an idea about how Jesus viewed violence? (If you need a hint, check out Matthew 19, John 2, or John 11.)

(talk)

Pretend you are with some friends who start talking about God.
Read their viewpoints and follow the instructions below.

CHRISTINA

It's hard to defend how angry God gets. You can see it
in the Old Testament. Those stories are really brutal
– it makes me sometimes wonder how we can follow a God
like that. I heard someone say once that the evil things
Christians have done in human history are just people
imitating what they saw God do in the Old Testament. We say
we hate Adolf Hitler who killed all those people. Hasn't
God done the same thing? How do we justify that?

THOMAS

God is real, but I think he is kind of "distant." It's
not that God is so cruel and mean. He's just not around.
Those stories in the Old Testament were just the people's
perceptions of what God wanted. He didn't really want them
to kill the Amalekites, but the people used God as an
excuse to do it. The truth is that God is not involved in
the everyday lives of human beings. He made the world and
then stepped back and let us make our own choices. When is
the last time you really saw God do something good or bad?

JANET

God is in my life doing good every day. Every breath, every
smile, every time I see something beautiful, I don't take
it for granted that God made those things and made me to
enjoy them. Jesus changed the world precisely by *not* being
violent. He showed God's true character. I will admit that
I don't understand all the Old Testament stories and they
seem confusing, but I know that was a different culture
than the world we live in today. I also know that Jesus has
earned my trust – I'm guessing there may be more to those
stories than I'll ever know.

CALVIN

I don't think people should question how God acts in the Bible so much. God's decisions are too hard for our little minds to understand. Doubting God about something like this will lead to doubt in other ways too. Why can't we just admit that we can't figure out everything God does and be okay with that?

Who do you relate to the *least*? Why?

What other questions do you have right now about this topic?

Session

8

*How can
I follow a
God who
would let
Christians
do such
bad things?*

It was game four of the World Series and the Chicago Cubs had a chance to sweep the Yankees.

As the game went on, the most important news stories of the evening scrolled by on the bottom of the screen. One news item read:

"Famous pastor admits to cheating on wife and stealing money from church – will face charges..."

Charley's friend Josh almost choked on a nacho chip.

"I'm so sick of these hypocritical Christians!" Josh yelled. "They are supposed to be these perfect people, but they're the ones who are doing the worst things."

Charley had gone to church for just over a year now, and thought the youth group was pretty fun. He was trying to learn about God, but it was easy to get confused by stuff like this. His friend Kirsten was the one who invited him to church. She was watching the game with them and chimed in.

"You need to calm down, Josh," she said. "Christians aren't perfect, they are just forgiven." *yes!*

"I'm sick of reading that stupid bumper sticker, and I think it's an excuse to behave badly," Josh said, growing visibly angry. "Think of all the terrible things that Christians have done over the course of history: The Crusades, The Spanish Inquisition, the killing of Native Americans, and slavery. Even Hitler said he was a Christian and that was one reason to get rid of the Jews. How can you possibly say you are one of *them*?"

The fun World Series viewing party had turned awkward.

"You have all your facts mixed up, Josh," she said. "Are you claiming to be perfect? Do you never make mistakes?"

"Of course I make mistakes," Josh replied. "But I don't need to use Jesus as an excuse for the dumb things I do."

Charley turned the television's volume all the way up as a humorous attempt at getting them to quit arguing. But he kept thinking about the conversation later. He didn't want to be associated with people who did horrible things.

Charley wondered, *"Why would God let Christians do such terrible things?"*

q *(questions)*

> When have you thought about this question before?

> While talking about the people who live in the slums or kids who are forced into labour and prostitution etc.

> What do you notice about the argument between Josh and Kirsten? Are they handling this conversation well? Why or why not?

Does Josh have his facts straight? What would you say to Josh?

Because Im not a historian im not sure but Im sure hes over exagerating. Id tell Josh that because of sin and Gods wish for his creation to have free will that homans are not always perfect and sometimes christians sin in a huge way

Talk to someone this week and ask them about this topic – preferably someone who may not consider themselves a Christian. How do they feel about this?

 *(notes)*

More Sides to the Story

While we can focus on some of the awful things done by Christians in history, those who have followed Jesus' lead have also been responsible for some incredible gifts to humanity. Consider these examples of issues where Christians have led the way in helping others: [8]

Children: *In ancient times, children were often not named for over a week in case the parents decided to dispose of the baby. The early Christian church helped change this practice because of Jesus' love for children (Matthew 19:14).*

Medical care: *Followers of Jesus founded many of the great health care systems in the world. Our hospitals, many of which are named after the disciples or characters in the scriptures (St. Luke's and Good Samaritan are common examples), are a reminder of that tradition. They were inspired by Jesus' words, "Whatever you do for the least of these, you do for me ..." (Matthew 25:40).*

Higher Learning: *Many of the world's greatest universities started with Jesus' teaching in mind. Schools like Oxford, Cambridge, Harvard, Stanford and Yale have their roots in Christianity. In fact, ninety-two percent of the first 138 universities founded in America were started by followers of Jesus. Jesus said, "Love the Lord Your God with all your... mind." (Luke 10:27).*

Slavery and Civil Rights: *Some of the greatest human rights leaders of our time, including William Wilberforce in England and Martin Luther King Jr. in the United States, passionately pursued racial equality because of Jesus' teaching. The apostle Paul wrote, "There is no longer Jew or Greek, there is no longer slave or free, there is no longer male and female; for all of you are one in Christ Jesus." (Galatians 3:28). Some people have called this the first written statement of human equality in all of human history.*

Look up: Christians & Collinization Origins.

Ethics: *"Humility" was not thought of as something positive in the time and culture Jesus lived in. Yet later Paul would write, "He humbled himself and became obedient to the point of death – even death on a cross." (Philippians 2:8). Jesus and the writers of the New Testament radically went against the ethic of taking revenge on others. Jesus said, "Love your enemies and pray for those who persecute you ..." (Matthew 5:44). The author of 1 Peter wrote, "Do not repay evil for evil or abuse for abuse; but, on the contrary, repay with a blessing." (1 Peter 3:9). The humility of Jesus has been the hallmark and inspiration of Christians like Mother Teresa (who served the poorest of the poor in Calcutta, India, for many years) and others who have sought to follow Jesus' example of serving rather than being served (see John 13 for a powerful story about Jesus washing his friends' feet).*

Join the Argument

Christians often spend time defending the terrible things some people have done in the name of Christianity. Instead of defending the actions of Christians who have done evil, it is often best to agree that those actions don't represent Jesus.

The Ironic Origin of the Word "Hypocrite"

Pastor and writer John Ortberg notes that the origin of the word "hypocrite" actually comes from Jesus himself. [9] Jesus uses that word 17 times in the New Testament. He constantly criticized religious leaders who said one thing, but did another. So sometimes it's totally appropriate to call out hypocrisy for what it is.

Mahatma Gandhi once said of Christianity: "I like your Christ, I do not like your Christians. Your Christians are so unlike your Christ." Is it possible to change the perception of Christians that many unchurched people have? How?

yes! Be the example.

S (*scripture*)

Jesus had a lot to say about how we live our lives. A disciple is someone who follows "the way" of someone else. Jesus invited us to be his disciples. He also warned that many people would claim to be his followers but were not genuine disciples. Read these words from Jesus' famous "Sermon on the Mount":

> *Watch out for false prophets. They come to you in sheep's clothing, but inwardly they are ferocious wolves. By their fruit you will recognize them. Do people pick grapes from thornbushes, or figs from thistles? Likewise, every good tree bears good fruit, but a bad tree bears bad fruit. A good tree cannot bear bad fruit, and a bad tree cannot bear good fruit. Every tree that does not bear good fruit is cut down and thrown into the fire. Thus, by their fruit you will recognize them.*
>
> — Matthew 7:15-20

Jesus says we will be able to tell false leaders "by their fruit." What do you think that means?

Galations 6

Have you ever experienced someone using Jesus or Christianity as a justification to do wrong?

Yes

Do you think people in the church can be easily led down the wrong path by false teaching? Why? How could that be prevented?

yes

BONUS Scripture...

The book of James in the New Testament stresses the importance of not just knowing about the way of Jesus. James encourages us to actually *live* like we know Jesus.

> *Do not merely listen to the word, and so deceive yourselves. Do what it says. Anyone who listens to the word but does not do what it says is like someone who looks at his face in a mirror and, after looking at himself, goes away and immediately forgets what he looks like. But whoever looks intently into the perfect law that gives freedom, and continues in it—not forgetting what they have heard, but doing it—they will be blessed in what they do.*   — James 1:22-25

What do you think is the main point of this passage?

Describe someone who lives in a way that makes it obvious they love Jesus. How do you think that person came to be that way?

Someone who has dedicated their life to serving and living for God.

(*talk*)

Pretend some friends post Facebook status updates like the ones below. Write your own short response in the comment boxes under each post.

Vicki

My professor today talked about the ways in which slave owners in the South cited passages in the Bible to justify keeping slaves. This was just one more example to me of how Christians have done terrible things. I sometimes wonder if the world would be a better place if there were no religions. Think about how many religious wars there have been!

Like · Comment · Share · 34 minutes ago

Jeremy

i'm embarrassed by the stupid things some people have done who claimed to be christians. but, i guess I've done some pretty dumb things too... i know we all need forgiveness. i just wish people could separate the teachings of Jesus from the bad things christians have done. i'm sad people are missing out on Jesus because they get stuck on christians' failures.

Like · Comment · Share · 2 minutes ago

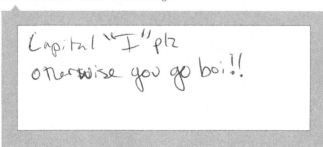

Capital "I" plz
otherwise you go boi!!

Henry

I'm tired of people saying that Christians are bad. Are you kidding me? Without Christians, the entire world as we know it would be a mess. Civilizations that have looked to Jesus as their source of ethics are far more advanced in civil rights than civilizations that haven't. I am happy to defend the record of Christians in history.

Like · Comment · Share · 41 minutes ago

> With out It the world wouldn't be? Hmm....

Joan

I see that Christians have done terrible things. I also see they have done good things. So... I don't understand why Christianity is necessary to live a good life. Some of the most ethical, wonderful people I know are not Christians. Shouldn't we just love each other regardless if someone is a Christian? why follow any religion? I can be ethical all by myself

Like · Comment · Share · 17 minutes ago

> Its not nesesary but having been saved by Jesus will give you an eternal life and something greater to live for than yourself

What's still bugging you about this topic?

10 Tips for reading your Bible

Hopefully this study has left you hungry to learn and grow more in your faith in God. One way to do that is by reading your Bible. Like anything worth doing, it takes some practice and time to know how to read it well. Here are a few tips on how you can get started or make your attempts at reading the Bible more meaningful.

1

Pray for the Spirit to Help You

You will not be able to understand the Bible well without God's help. Pray for the Holy Spirit to guide you when you read. Jesus told his followers, "When the Spirit of truth comes, he will guide you into all truth ..." (John 16:13). Take Jesus up on this promise and invite God to lead you. *Ask God to give you a heart that is open to being changed.*

Formation vs. Information

2

To read the Bible and grow from it, you need to learn a different way to read. In school, you usually read for "information." Reading for school often means you need to read as much as you can as fast as you can. Why? Two words: FINAL EXAM.

But reading the Bible is more about "formation" than information. God is using the Bible to shape or *form* you into a new person. That doesn't happen by reading as fast as you can and trying to memorize facts. With the Bible, it's often just the opposite. Read the Bible slowly. Pray as you go. Stop and ask questions. There is no pressure to "get through it." *If you are just trying to get through the Bible, the Bible won't get through to you.*

No Shame

High school is often the first time people start to feel shame that they don't know much about the Bible. Don't fall into the trap of thinking everyone knows how to read the Bible except you. Many adults, probably even those who go to your church, don't know how to read it well.

Sometimes high schoolers feel like they are so "far behind" when it comes to Bible knowledge that they don't even try. Don't be afraid to be honest about what you do and don't understand about the Bible, and ask for help from a trusted leader (see #7 below).

Get a Readable Bible

Did you know there are all kinds of Bible translations out there? Make sure your Bible has words that are easily understandable. The King James Version may not be your best choice, because it was translated in a language popular centuries ago. Some translations that are easier for students to read include the *New International Version* (NIV), *Common English Bible* (CEB), *New Revised Standard Version* (NRSV), or the *New Living Translation* (NLT). You might also want to look for a Bible that has extra notes for context, sometimes called a "Study Bible." Some of these are written especially for teenagers. Most of the excerpts in this study have been from the NIV translation, with a few from *The Message* (which utilizes modern phrases and expressions to communicate in today's language as much as possible).

Don't Start at Start

Jim remembers getting his first Bible, opening it, and starting to read it just like every book he'd ever read; from the beginning to the end. He made it to Exodus before he quit. If you've never read the Bible before, *you may not want to start in Genesis.* Read one of the gospels first (Matthew, Mark, Luke, or John). Those books tell Jesus' story and are a great place to get started. Then go back and get a sense for the bigger story from Creation to New Creation (Genesis to Revelation).

6

Read the Notes Before the Book

A good Bible will often include notes that introduce each book. It is good to read those notes before you dive in. Bibles with a good introduction will help you understand the context of what you are reading. Context is important because it tells you who is writing to whom and why they are writing.

Bible Reading is a "Team Sport"

When you begin reading the Bible, you will be confused at times. *That is okay.* Read with someone else who knows the Bible more than you do. Find a pastor at your church, another Christian group leader, a parent or a friend who knows the Bible and can help you. Don't struggle through the Bible on your own!

Use Your Imagination **8**

The Bible tells some of the greatest stories you'll ever read. It also does not always elaborate on important elements of those stories. Stop when you read stories in the Bible and ask questions like, "What was the person thinking and feeling? What would it have been like to be there?" Use your imagination when you read the Bible.

Stick With it   **10**

Many people start the Bible, get confused, and quit. Don't let that be you. If you are confused, remember that you're not alone. Reading the Bible is much like learning to play an instrument or a new sport. The more you practice reading it, the more natural it will become. Don't give up.

It's About God **9**

The Bible is not a "nice road map" with good tips on how to live. The Bible is a collection of stories, poems, songs, and letters that work together to tell one big story about God and about us. There *are* great thoughts about living your life, but the goal of the Bible is to reveal God, and to draw you into a relationship with God. Get to know God as you read it.

Insider Tips

⊗ There are two major sections of the Bible: The Old and New Testaments. The Old Testament tells the story of creation, of the journeys of God's people, and of their anticipation of the coming of Jesus. It also includes books like the Psalms, which capture poetry and songs that span the breadth of human emotion and response to God. The New Testament tells the story of Jesus on earth and what his life, death and resurrection mean. It goes on to share about the earliest churches and some of their letters to one another about living out the way of Jesus together. It closes with visions of Jesus returning to make all things new, and a promise that he will bring those visions to reality some day.

⊗ The Bible is broken into chapters and verses. John 3:16 refers to a verse in the gospel of John, chapter 3, verse 16. The little numbers you find in the midst of the paragraphs and sentences are verse numbers and make things easier to find. Many Bibles include footnotes that refer you to other passages where you find a similar verse, idea, or an exact quote that is repeated by another author. Sometimes that can help you piece together the different parts of the story.

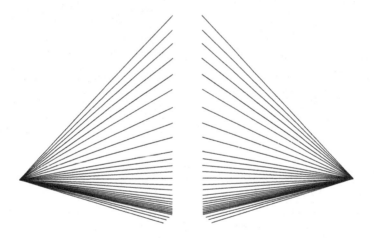

⊗ The Gospels are the four books that start the New Testament (Matthew, Mark, Luke, and John) and tell the story of Jesus. The word *gospel* means "good news."

Footnotes

1. This list and the telephone viewpoint are compiled from various sources and represent the thoughts of New Testament scholars such as Bart Ehrman. See ehrmanblog.org or Bart Ehrman, *Misquoting Jesus: The Story Behind Who Changed the Bible and Why* (San Francisco: HarperOne, 2007).

2. From a lecture in 2007 at Stanford University titled *"Misquoting Jesus, Stanford Lecture, How the Bible Got Tainted."*

3. F. F. Bruce, *The New Testament Documents: Are They Reliable?* 15.

4. C.S. Lewis, *Mere Christianity* (New York: Macmillan Publishing, 1942), 121.

5. John MacArthur, *The Battle for the Beginning* (Nashville: Thomas Nelson, 2001), 29.

6. Paine, Thomas. *The Age of Reason*. Ed. Kerry Walters (Peterborough: Broadview Press, 2011), Part 1, Section IV.

7. Dawkins, Richard. *The God Delusion* (New York: Houghton Mifflin, 2006), 31.

8. These summaries are adapted from John Ortberg's *Who is This Man?: The Unpredictable Impact of the Inescapable Jesus.* (Grand Rapids: Zondervan, 2012).

9. John Ortberg, *Who is this Man?* (Grand Rapids: Zondervan, 2012), 119.

Photos

Photo credits, in order of appearance

Section 0

Blue whale by Flickr user mikebaird.
New Student Orientation Fall 2013 84 by
Flickr user COD Newsroom.
n156_w1150 by Flickr user biodivlibrary.

Section 1

Prove your existence. by Flickr user
W3155Y.
into the promise land by Flickr user
Patrick Feller.
Hope by Juan Fernández.
⬜ by Juan Fernández.
Colossians 1:16-42 from earlybible.com/
manuscripts.

Section 2

Pages&pages. by Flickr user W3155Y.
Self-portrait by Juan Fernández.
Meant to live by Juan Fernández.
J U S T I C E by Juan Fernández.
× ô × by Juan Fernández.
Abandoned Farmhouse by Flickr user
Ben K Adams.

Session 3

Charles Darwin by darvinci.
Teaching Chemistry by Flickr user
starmanseries.
duck lizard by Flickr user valanzola.t.
Lamellae by Flickr user Furryscaly.
View from Plane, BC June 2010 by Flickr
user anitakhart.
Spiral Galaxy by Flickr user Jsome1.

Session 4

Amy. by Flickr user W3155Y.
Untitled by Flickr user martinak15.
Untitled by Flickr user martinak15.
278/365 by Flickr user martinak15.
223/365 And our journey is over. by Flickr
user martinak15.
Majestic. by Flickr user W3155Y.

Fly away by Flickr user 55Laney69.
Kira. by Flickr user W3155Y.
The Lost Traveler by Flickr user
martinak15.
Island. by Flickr user W3155Y.

Session 5

Eden Project by Flickr user Ben K Adams.
London Central Mosque by Flickr user
AwayWeGo210.
Decorative Sculpture at the entrance of
Sri Krishnan Temple, Singapore.
elyana by Flickr user -syauqee-.
Coexist by unknown.
Golden Buddha Statue by Fickr user
epSos.de.
Monks Queuing by Flickr user
Schwarzkaefer.
Prayer flags by Flickr user scjody.

Session 6

The EV by Flickr user W3155Y.
sleepy head. by Flickr user W3155Y.
Leap of Faith by Flickr user
ClickFlashPhotos / Nicki Varkevisser
Lugares lejanos. by Olga Ferrer Saladié.
Birds by Matthew Schuler.
Con mi amigo Dariel nomas by Flickr user
Irving Abdiel.

Session 7

Skeleton. by Flickr user W3155Y.
M119 howitzer by unknown.
M E R C Y by Juan Fernández.
Nuclear bomb explosion by unknown.
Wasser über Deck und Luken WNA by
Buonasera.
Homage to banksy by unknown.
D800 100% Moon crop by Flickr user
Nick-K (Nikos Koutoulas).
Atomic Bomb Explosion Military by
unknown.
Blue. by Flickr user W3155Y.
Kendall. by Flickr user W3155Y.
The 1960s⬜Riot police by Flickr user
panDx1.
Eden Project by Flickr user Ben K Adams.